Revised and Updated

Ohio History

Marcia Schonberg

Heinemann Library
Chicago, Illinois

www.heinemannraintree.com
Visit our website to find out more information about Heinemann-Raintree books.

To order:

☎ Phone 888-454-2279

💻 Visit www.heinemannraintree.com to browse our catalog and order online.

©2003, 2010 Heinemann Library
an imprint of Capstone Global Library, LLC
Chicago, Illinois

Edited by Megan Cotugno
Designed by Kim Miracle
Photo research by Tracy Cummins
Originated by Heinemann Library
Printed in China by Leo Paper Products Ltd.

13 12 11 10 09
10 9 8 7 6 5 4 3 2 1

New edition ISBNs: 978-1-4329-2570-3 (hardcover)
978-1-4329-2577-2 (paperback)

Library of Congress Cataloging-in-Publication Data
Schonberg, Marcia.
  Ohio history / Marcia Schonberg.
    v. cm. -- (Heinemann state studies)
Includes bibliographical references (p.) and index.
Contents: The frontier era -- The territorial era -- The early statehood era -- Industrial expansion -- Prohibition, the Great Depression, and World War II -- Toward the new millenium.
  ISBN 1-4034-0666-9 (HC) -- ISBN 1-4034-2689-9 (PB)
  1. Ohio--History--Juvenile literature. [1. Ohio--History.] I. Title.
II. Series.
  F491.3.S366 2003
  977.1--dc21
                    2002154203

Acknowledgments

The author and publishers are grateful to the following for permission to reproduce copyright material: **pp. 4, 13T, 17, 20, 23, 25, 27, 28, 29, 30, 37, 40** The Ohio Historical Society; **p. 5** Ohio State Museum/Werner Forman/Art Resource, NY; **p. 6** Richard A. Cooke/Corbis; **pp. 7, 11, 19, 22, 44** maps.com/Heinemann Library; **p. 9** North Wind Picture Archives; **pp. 11, 12, 13B, 16, 24, 33T, 42** The Granger Collection; **pp. 14, 26** Brown Brothers; **p. 21** Kevin Parsons/Alamy; **p. 39** Scott Swanson/Hulton Archive/Getty Images; **p. 41** R. Gates/Getty Images; **p. 43** Tricia Cunningham/Ohio Bicentennial Commission

Cover photograph of State Street in 1901, Columbus, Ohio reproduced with permission of ©Corbis.

Every effort has been made to contact copyright holders of any material reproduced in this book. Any omissions will be rectified in subsequent printings if notice is given to the publisher.

All the Internet addresses (URLs) given in this book were valid at the time of going to press. However, due to the dynamic nature of the Internet, some addresses may have changed, or sites may have changed or ceased to exist since publication. While the author and Publishers regret any inconvenience this may cause readers, no responsibility for any such changes can be accepted by either the author or the Publishers.

Contents

Some words are shown in bold, **like this**. You can find out what they mean by looking in the glossary.

Early Ohio, Beginning–1783

The story of Ohio begins long before Ohio became a state. Ohio's earliest settlers were **prehistoric** people, called Paleo-Indians. They did not leave written records to tell us how they lived, but they did leave other clues behind, such as bones, pottery, and tools. Scientists called **archaeologists** learn about the past by studying these **artifacts** and the places where these people lived.

Paleo-Indians, 13,000 BCE

Paleo-Indians came to the area that is now Ohio about 15,000 years ago. They hunted **mastodons** and **woolly mammoths** and gathered berries and nuts from the trees. This is why archaeologists call Paleo-Indians hunters and gatherers. When the giant animals became **extinct**, the Paleo-Indians disappeared, too.

These Ohio Paleo-Indian spear points are from ca. 9000 BCE and show a variety of shapes and types of stone.

Archaic Indians, 8000 BCE

People of the Archaic Period first lived in Ohio around 8000 BCE. They hunted animals such as deer and caribou and fished in Ohio's many rivers, cooking the animals over a fire. Archaic Indians lived in small communities and made tools from bones, shells, and **flint**. Archaic hunters used a spear thrower called an **atlatl**, which made hunting easier. The Archaic people disappeared like the Paleo-Indians, but archaeologists do not know why.

Woodland Indians, 1000 BCE

The Adena and Hopewell Indians are called Mound Builders, because they built dirt mounds covered with stones and grass. Archaeologists think they lived throughout Ohio, since many mounds have been discovered around the state. They think the mounds were used for protection, in cemeteries, and for festivals. Some mounds faced the sun, probably so the ancient people could predict seasons based on the length of shadows.

This Hopewell pipe in the form of a toad is between 1,500 and 2,300 years old and can be seen at the Ohio State Museum.

Serpent Mound, in Locust Grove, Ohio, is the largest serpent-shaped mound in the United States. It is 405 meters (1,330 feet) long, about 0.9 meter (3 feet) high, and was probably made by the Adena people.

Late Prehistoric Indians, 200 CE

Fort Ancients and Whittlesey people came to Ohio around 200 CE. The Fort Ancients settled in southwestern Ohio, near present-day Lebanon, and further east in Ross County. The Whittlesey People settled in northeastern Ohio. Both groups lived in villages, planted gardens, and hunted with bows and arrows. They may have lived in Ohio as late as the 1600s, close to the time of early European settlement in America.

Historic Indians, 1700

We know a lot more about historic Native Americans, because soon after they came to Ohio around 1700, early European explorers arrived. These explorers kept records in journals and described the Native Americans they met. Most of the information we have about Ohio's Native Americans comes from the written records of European explorers and settlers.

The six historic Native American tribes that lived in Ohio were the Ottawa, Wyandot, Mingo, Miami, Shawnee, and Delaware. They moved west into what would become Ohio when they lost their lands on the east coast to European settlers and other tribes, especially the Iroquois. Ohio had plenty of forests, lakes, and rivers to fulfill their needs. These Native Americans lived near rivers and made canoes from trees for transportation. Each tribe had its own **culture** and language.

The Native Americans of Ohio and the surrounding region did not always stay in the exact same place. However, this map gives an idea of where main villages and hunting grounds of Ohio tribes were located at the time when European and American settlers were coming to the region.

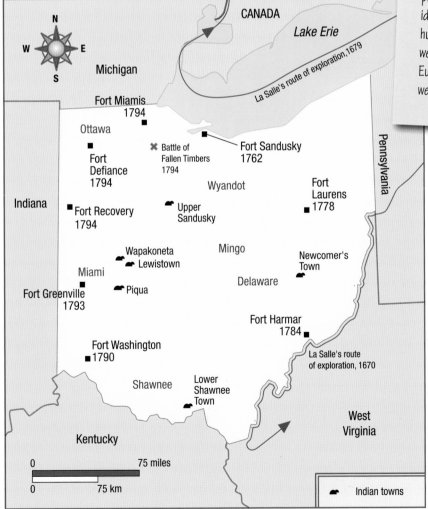

European Contact, 1670–1794

Europeans Arrive

A Frenchman named Louis Jolliet was the first known European fur trader and explorer on Lake Erie in 1669. Around 1670, another Frenchman, named René-Robert Cavelier, Sieur de la Salle, came upon the Ohio River. He was probably the first European to reach present-day Ohio. He claimed all of the land he saw for France.

By the end of the 1600s, the British had successful colonies on the Atlantic Coast. The British also claimed all the **territory** extending west from those colonies, including what would later become Ohio. Some English traders and explorers traveled around Ohio at the end of the 1600s. As long as large amounts of people were not settling the area, it seemed the French and British could share it. The Native Americans of Ohio exchanged bear, deer, and fox **pelts** for beads, guns, knives, cloth, blankets, and alcohol from the Europeans. French trappers in the area especially profited from the fur trade.

Ohio Company of Virginia, 1751

In 1747 English settlers and Virginians organized a company called the Ohio Company of Virginia. Their plan was to **colonize** the Ohio region. In 1750, the Ohio Company sent the Englishman Christopher Gist to explore the upper Ohio River Valley. With the English trying to colonize Ohio and other areas west of their colonies on the East Coast, more conflicts between the British and French broke out. They were fighting for the same territory, and both claimed ownership of the land. When fighting broke out, the Native Americans of Ohio usually sided with the French. This was because the French only seemed to want to trade with the Native Americans, while the British wanted to settle on their lands.

French and Indian War, 1754–1763

The British and French went to war over territory in America, including the Ohio region, in 1754. Most of the fighting in the French and Indian War occurred east of the Ohio region. The war ended with the Treaty of Paris in 1763. In the treaty, France gave Great Britain all of its land east of the Mississippi River except New Orleans. The British were now free to colonize the Ohio region. As more and more British settlers moved into Ohio, the Native Americans struggled to survive. The British forced the Native Americans to leave their land or try to become part of the society of the white settlers.

When fighting broke out over the Ohio region in the French and Indian War, George Washington, then a British/Virginian officer, was sent to the Ohio Valley to convince the French to leave.

Revolutionary War, 1775–1783

War broke out in America again in 1775. The American colonists wanted freedom from British rule and signed the Declaration of Independence in 1776. As with the French and Indian War, most of the fighting took place east of the Ohio region. However, George Rogers Clark led colonial troops to victories over the British in the area of Ohio. In 1780 Clark defeated the Shawnee, who were **allies** of the British, in the Battle of Piqua, near present-day Springfield, Ohio.

The Treaty of Paris, signed in 1783, recognized the independence of the United States and extended its territory west to the Mississippi River, north to Canada, east to the Atlantic Ocean, and south to about Florida. The Ohio region now belonged to the United States.

Northwest Territory, 1787–1802

In 1787 Ohio became part of the Northwest **Territory**, which was created by the U.S. Congress. The Northwest **Ordinance** of 1787 set up parts of the Northwest Territory to eventually become states, including Ohio. It also made slavery illegal in the Northwest Territory. The Northwest Ordinance allowed for the U.S. government to oversee territories that were not yet states. It also helped make those territories more attractive to new settlers, who began coming west to settle Ohio and other regions.

Ohio and the Northwest Territory

The Northwest Territory eventually became the five states of Ohio, Indiana, Illinois, Michigan, and Wisconsin. Marietta, Ohio, was the first capital of the Northwest Territory.

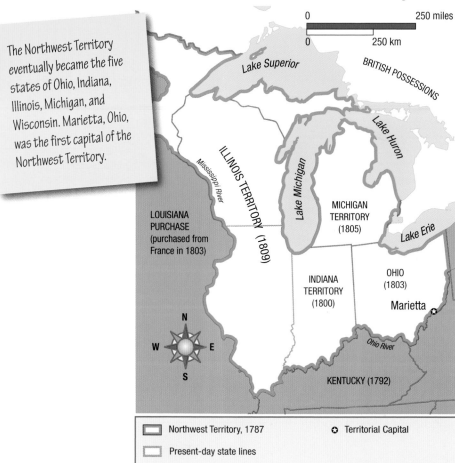

0 — 250 miles
0 — 250 km

Lake Superior

BRITISH POSSESSIONS

Lake Huron

Lake Michigan

ILLINOIS TERRITORY (1809)

Mississippi River

LOUISIANA PURCHASE (purchased from France in 1803)

MICHIGAN TERRITORY (1805)

Lake Erie

INDIANA TERRITORY (1800)

OHIO (1803)

Marietta

Ohio River

KENTUCKY (1792)

N W E S

Northwest Territory, 1787

Present-day state lines

Territorial Capital

Marietta, 1788

The Ohio Company of Associates was organized in Boston, Massachusetts, in 1786. As another part of the Northwest Ordinance of 1787, the U.S. Congress granted the Ohio Company of Associates land in what is now southeastern Ohio. The Ohio Company of Associates founded Marietta on April 7, 1788. It was the first permanent white settlement in Ohio, located where the Muskingum and Ohio rivers joined. Rufus Putnam, a Revolutionary War general, was the leader of the colony. On July 15, 1788, Northwest Territory governor Arthur St. Clair made Marietta the **capital** of the Northwest Territory.

Northwest Ordinance

The Northwest Ordinance of 1787 set up three steps that a territory had to go through in order to become a state. These steps were:

1) U.S. Congress appointed a governor, secretary, and three judges for the territory.

2) Once the territory had at least 5,000 adult men living there, it could choose a **legislature** and send a delegate to the U.S. Congress who could speak but not vote.

3) When the total population of the territory reached 60,000, it could apply for admission into the Union.

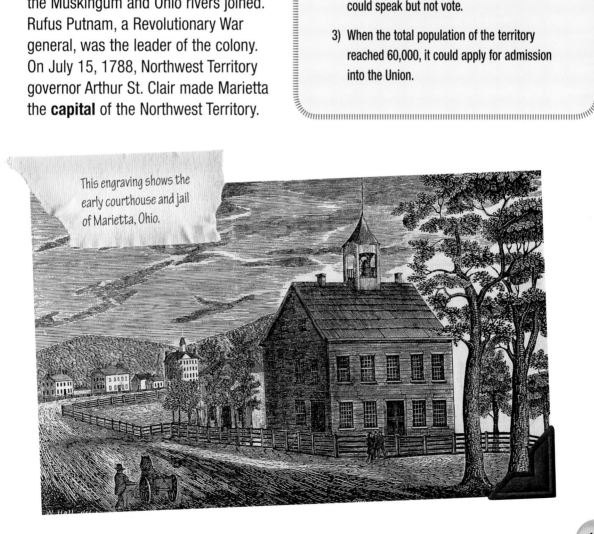

This engraving shows the early courthouse and jail of Marietta, Ohio.

Soon other communities developed along the Ohio River. Many settlers were Revolutionary War **veterans** who received land in the Northwest Territory as payment for their military service. In 1788 settlers founded a village called Losantiville, which Governor St. Clair renamed Cincinnati in 1790. Ohio's settler population was growing, and this brought more trouble with the Native Americans of the area.

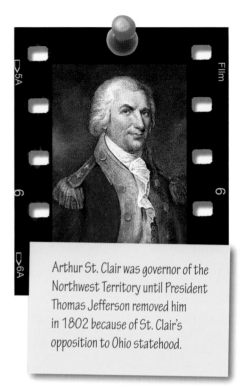

Arthur St. Clair was governor of the Northwest Territory until President Thomas Jefferson removed him in 1802 because of St. Clair's opposition to Ohio statehood.

Battle of Fallen Timbers, 1794

Native Americans in the Ohio region fought back against the colonists moving into their lands. In 1791 Little Turtle of the Miami and Blue Jacket of the Shawnee led warriors of several tribes, including the Shawnee, Miami, Delaware, and Ottawa, against General (and Governor) St. Clair and his soldiers. A battle took place near Fort Hamilton in Ohio, and the Indians easily won.

President George Washington forced St. Clair to resign from the army and sent Major General "Mad Anthony" Wayne to Ohio to fight the Native Americans. When Little Turtle heard about Wayne's arrival, Little Turtle decided he should make peace. He then turned over his leadership to Blue Jacket. In August 1794, Blue Jacket and 2,000 warriors attacked Wayne and his American troops near what is now Toledo, Ohio. The two forces met in a field full of fallen trees knocked down by a tornado. As a result, the fight became known as the Battle of Fallen Timbers. The Native Americans were defeated in this battle.

Ohio Native Americans never recovered from their loss at the Battle of Fallen Timbers. In 1795 General Wayne forced the defeated people to sign the Treaty of Greenville. The Native Americans gave up most of their land when they signed the treaty.

This painting of the Treaty of Greenville shows Chief Little Turtle presenting a belt to General Anthony Wayne while William Wells translates. The painting hangs in the Ohio statehouse today.

They were sent to live in northern Ohio in an area known as the Black Swamp. It was an area the settlers did not want because it was too wet to settle and farm. The Treaty of Greenville ended Native American resistance in Ohio. It led to the removal of Ohio's native peoples to **reservations** in Kansas and Oklahoma. Nearly all Native Americans who lived in the Ohio region were forced to move west within 40 years.

With the fighting over, more settlers moved into the Ohio region. In 1795 a man named Jonathon Dayton planned a town where the Mad and Miami rivers meet. He named the town Dayton, after himself. The Connecticut **surveyor** Moses Cleaveland founded the village of Cleveland in 1796.

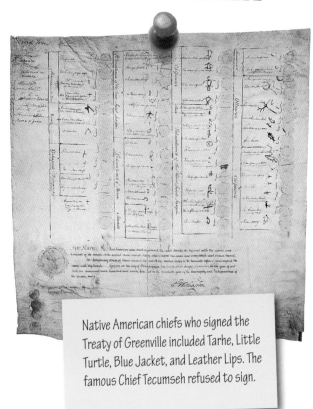

Native American chiefs who signed the Treaty of Greenville included Tarhe, Little Turtle, Blue Jacket, and Leather Lips. The famous Chief Tecumseh refused to sign.

Statehood and Growth, 1803-1900

In 1800 the U.S. Congress passed the Division Act. This act created the Indiana **Territory** out of the western part of the Northwest Territory. The remaining eastern part was still called the Northwest Territory, and a town named Chillicothe now became the **capital**. In November 1802, a convention in Chillicothe wrote the first **constitution** for Ohio. Thomas Worthington led the convention, and so later became known as the Father of Ohio Statehood. Ohio had a population of about 70,000 at the time, more than the 60,000 necessary to be considered for statehood. On March 1, 1803, Ohio became the 17th state when its **legislature** met for the first time. Edward Tiffin was chosen as the first governor.

Thomas Worthington served as a U.S. Senator for Ohio and later as governor of the state.

Ohio Capitals

Ohio's capital changed to Zanesville in 1810, then back to Chillicothe in 1812 while a new capital was chosen in the center of the state. The Ohio legislature decided to build a new city, Columbus, on the banks of the Scioto River. Columbus became the permanent capital of Ohio in 1816.

Expanding Trade, 1803

In 1803 Thomas Jefferson bought the Louisiana Territory from France in what became known as the Louisiana Purchase. The United States now owned the land between the Mississippi River and the Rocky Mountains, going from the Gulf of Mexico to the Canadian border. The Louisiana Purchase helped Ohio settlers, because they could now ship goods from the Ohio River down the Mississippi River to the port of New Orleans. River trade with New Orleans soon thrived.

Steamboats

The *New Orleans* was the first steamboat to travel down the Ohio River all the way to New Orleans, Louisiana, in 1811. The success of the voyage opened the way for further use of steamboats, which quickly became the favorite mode of transportation and shipping on U.S. rivers.

War of 1812 (1812–1815)

Even though the United States won its independence from Great Britain by winning the Revolutionary War, the British did not respect the new country. The British were still interested in the land and **resources** of North America and continued to keep soldiers in regions claimed by the United States. Great Britain also attacked U.S. ships and kidnapped sailors. The British also encouraged Native Americans in Ohio and the Northwest Territory to raid property and attack American settlers. For all of these reasons, the United States once again went to war with Great Britain in 1812. Two important battles of the war took place in Ohio and its waters.

On May 1, 1813, the British army attacked Fort Meigs, located on the Maumee River in present-day Perrysburg, Ohio. U.S. General William Henry Harrison was ready with a strong fort and 1,200 troops. Harrison held the fort, and on May 9, 1813, the British gave up and left in defeat. This was an important victory for the United States in Ohio and the Northwest region.

This 19th-century engraving shows Oliver Hazard Perry leaving his badly damaged ship, the *Lawrence*, for the *Niagara* to continue fighting against the British at the Battle of Lake Erie.

Also in 1813, Commodore Oliver H. Perry sailed his U.S. fleet from South Bass Island off the Ohio shore to fight a British fleet in the western part of Lake Erie. The Battle of Lake Erie took place on September 10, 1813. After a tough fight and the loss of his ship, the *Lawrence*, the British fleet surrendered to Commodore Perry. The United States controlled the Great Lakes, an important transportation route, after this important battle.

The Treaty of Ghent, signed in Ghent, Belgium, in 1814, officially ended the War of 1812. However, because news traveled slowly in those days, fighting still took place in 1815, before news of the treaty reached all of the battlefields in the United States. The Treaty of Ghent contained 11 articles that explained in detail the conditions of the first article. *Article I* of the treaty stated: "There shall be a ... peace between His Britannic Majesty and the United States, ... All hostilities, both by sea and land, shall cease as soon as this treaty shall have been ratified by both parties, ... All territory, ... taken by either party from the other during the war, ... shall be **restored** without delay.... "

Transportation Allows Growth

After the War of 1812, the U.S. government forced the few Native Americans still living in northwest Ohio to leave for Kansas and Oklahoma. With peace secured and the threat of Native American raids gone, thousands of people from the eastern states moved to Ohio. They came from New England, New York, and Pennsylvania. **Immigrants** also came from Great Britain and Germany to start new lives in Ohio.

The nation's first real highway, called the National Road, reached St. Clairsville, Ohio, in 1825. The starting point for the National Road was located in Cumberland, Maryland. The National Road made it easier for people from the east to come to Ohio. Before the National Road, it was difficult to travel through the mountains in the east and across streams and rivers. The National Road included bridges, which made the westward journey easier for settlers traveling by wagon, horseback, or foot. Farmers and manufacturers could also transport their goods more easily to different markets along the National Road.

This photo shows the National Road being paved in the early 1900s. Before that, in the 1800s, it was a smooth dirt road, which would have made travel difficult in wet weather.

Between 1825 and 1845, several **canals** opened, providing a water transportation system for Ohio. With the completion of the canals, goods could be more easily transported from the Atlantic Coast, through Ohio, and then south to New Orleans. The Erie Canal opened in 1825. It went through the state of New York, connecting Lake Erie with the East Coast and Atlantic Ocean. The Ohio and Erie Canal was completed in 1832. This canal linked Cleveland in northern Ohio with Portsmouth in southern Ohio. The Miami and Erie Canal was completed in 1845. It linked

Canals and the National Road, 1850

New canals connected northern Ohio and Lake Erie to southern Ohio and the Ohio River, and the National Road connected eastern and western Ohio. These new advances in transportation set the stage for Ohio's tremendous economic and population growth.

Toledo and Cincinnati. Both of these Ohio canals linked Lake Erie in the north with the Ohio River in the south. The canals were busy trade routes. They brought jobs and money to Ohio and helped the state grow.

Since Ohio is situated between the East Coast and the cities of Chicago and St. Louis, goods traveling east and west had to pass through the state. When rail lines were built, it was cheaper and faster to transport goods by rail than over land or by canal. Since goods had to pass through the state to move east or west, Ohio needed railroad lines. The first railroad in Ohio was constructed in 1836. By 1850 there were 481 kilometers (299 miles) of railroad track in the state. By 1860 Ohio had almost 4,828 kilometers (3,000 miles) of track, which was more than any other state in the nation at the time.

With canals and railroads linking Ohio's cities with sources of raw materials and other cities in the east and west, Ohio became a center of **industry**. As a result, its economy grew quickly. As industries grew in Ohio's cities, more people moved to those cities looking for work, and Ohio's population continued to grow and become more **urban**.

Building Canals

Many Irish and German immigrants came to Ohio to find work digging the canals. They responded to ads like this one (below) from the *Cleveland Herald* in 1829. It was a hard and dangerous job, and the workers were only paid about 30 cents a day, which is equal to about 6 dollars today.

LABOURERS WANTED ON THE OHIO CANAL.

THE subscribers wish to employ on the canal, near Bethlehem, Stark County, *Two Hundred* labourers, to whom good wages, (from 11 to 12 dollars per month,) prompt pay and good fare will be given.
SWEET & WOOD.
Bethlehem, April, 1829.   9-t

LABOURERS WANTED.

I Want to hire **40** good hands to work, on Lock Pit No. 44, until completed, to commence immediately.
JOHN A. ACKLEY.
Cleaveland. April 16, 1829.   93-3

LABOURERS WANTED.

FROM fifteen to twenty labourers will find immediate employ on

Canal Traffic

A system of **locks** raised and lowered the water in canals to keep them deep enough for the boats to pass. Different types of boats had different purposes. Packet boats carried passengers. Boats hauling cargo, or goods, were called freighters. State boats were owned by the state and helped to maintain the canals.

This photo shows a boat moving along the Ohio and Erie Canal south of Cleveland in the late 1800s.

Cities such as Cleveland, Youngstown, and Cincinnati, for instance, grew quickly as industrial centers. Coal was discovered in Youngstown in 1845 and was used to fuel the blast furnaces of iron factories. This allowed the iron industry to boom in northeast Ohio, including Cleveland. Cleveland was perfect for shipping out the iron produced, with a large harbor on Lake Erie. In southwest Ohio, Cincinnati, with its location on the Ohio River, became a center for shipping and meatpacking, especially of pork. By the 1850s, Cincinnati workers were slaughtering and packing more than 400,000 hogs a year. At that time, Cincinnati was the sixth largest city in the United States. From 1800 to 1850, the population of Ohio went from 45,000 to almost 2 million, ranking it third in the nation in population after New York and Pennsylvania.

A Free State

Ohio was growing, but residents worried about slavery in the South. The Northwest **Ordinance** of 1787 said that none of the states carved from the Northwest Territory could have slaves. By 1817 **abolitionists** began to meet. They called for an end to slavery.

Even though Ohio was a free state, it had laws against helping slaves. These were Ohio's Black Laws, passed in 1804. In 1850 the **Fugitive** Slave Law of the United States made it a crime to help slaves. Although there were no slaves in Ohio, laws and **prejudice** kept African Americans from being treated equally with whites. Because of these laws, some free African Americans left Ohio to live in Canada. In addition, many Ohio abolitionists helped escaped slaves on their way to Canada, where they would be free.

Society of Friends

The Society of Friends is more commonly known as the Quakers. Many Quakers came to Ohio in the late 1700s and early 1800s, settling in southern and eastern Ohio. They started communities, such as Mt. Pleasant and Alliance. The Quakers believe God exists in all humans of every race. They strongly disliked slavery and actively participated in the **Underground Railroad**. They also spoke out against slavery. Quakers in Mt. Pleasant published two antislavery newspapers beginning in the early 1800s—the *Philanthropist* and the *Genius of Universal Emancipation*. First published in 1817, the *Philanthropist* was the first antislavery newspaper in the United States.

Reverend John Rankin

One of the most famous Ohioans who helped slaves find freedom was Reverend John Rankin. Reverend Rankin was a Presbyterian minister. He came to Ohio from Tennessee, a slave state. He saw the way slaves were bought and sold like farm animals, and he decided he had to do something. He wrote letters that were published, and he formed an antislavery society. He traveled in Ohio to convince other churches to join. By 1837 there were more than 200 antislavery societies in Ohio. From 1822 to 1865, Rankin and his family helped hundreds of escaped slaves in their journey to freedom. The Rankin home (right) was located on the Ohio River in Ripley, Ohio. John Parker, a Ripley abolitionist and former slave, wrote of the Rankin house: "A lighted candle stood as a beacon which could be seen from across the river, and like the North Star was the guide to the fleeing slave."

Ohio had many antislavery supporters. Most supporters wanted to stop slavery peacefully, but some did not. John Brown was willing to fight to free slaves. John Brown lived in Akron and came from a family of abolitionists. He hated slavery and hoped to start a slave rebellion in the South. In 1859, Brown led a group of 22 men to Harper's Ferry, Virginia, where they hoped to steal guns from the U.S. **arsenal**. Brown was captured, tried for **treason**, and hanged. Before his hanging, hundreds of Ohioans who agreed with Brown's feelings against slavery traveled to Virginia to visit him.

John Parker

John Parker was born to a slave in Virginia in 1827. When he was eight years old, he was sold to a doctor. He was a house boy. He had a better life than the slaves who worked in the fields. Parker learned to read and write and knew he wanted to help slaves find freedom someday. Luckily for him, he was sent to an iron **foundry** to work. When he was sold again, he was allowed to keep the money he earned in the factory. He bought his freedom with his savings and left for Ohio. There, he heard of Reverend Rankin's work and went to Ripley, Ohio, to help. He made many daring rescues and helped many fugitives escape.

Underground Railroad

Abolitionists in Ohio worked to help escaped slaves make it to the North and to Canada to gain their freedom. Many Ohioans were part of a secret network called the Underground Railroad. The Underground Railroad was not an actual railroad with a train, nor was it actually underground. It consisted of a number of people around the country, especially in the North, who helped escaped slaves. These people hid slaves in their homes and businesses, giving them food and aid, and helping them to move north quickly and avoid capture. The people who helped the escaped slaves on the Underground Railroad were known as conductors. The safe houses, where slaves could find food and shelter, were known as stations.

Underground Railroad in Ohio

Due to its location, probably two of every five runaway slaves on the Underground Railroad came through Ohio, usually on their way to Canada, where slavery was illegal. This map shows some of the most traveled Ohio routes on the Underground Railroad.

Some of the most traveled routes of the Underground Railroad ran through Ohio. If escaped slaves could make it from Kentucky or Virginia north across the Ohio River into Ohio, they were in free territory. However, they still had to worry about the 1850 Fugitive Slave Law, so staying in Ohio was risky. Many escaped slaves made their way through Ohio, up to Detroit, and to Canada from there, where slavery was illegal throughout the country. Others traveled by boat across Lake Erie, leaving from Sandusky, Ohio, and other ports. It is thought that as many as 100,000 slaves escaped through the Underground Railroad, and 40,000 of those came through Ohio, making it the most traveled route. The Ohioans who helped escaped slaves on the Underground Railroad risked imprisonment, large fines, or worse if they were discovered.

The increased use and success of the Underground Railroad further angered Southern slave owners. It showed that African Americans and many whites were determined to end slavery in the United States. This added to the hostility between the North and South that led to the Civil War.

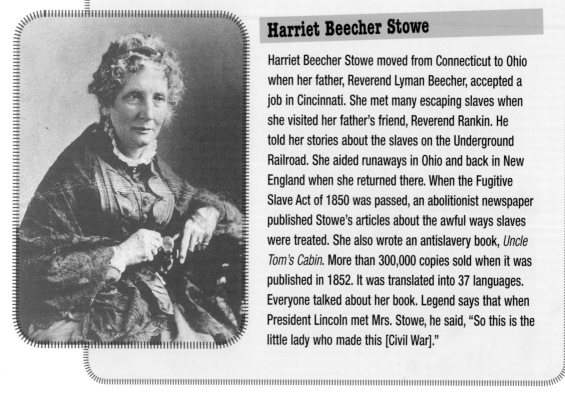

Harriet Beecher Stowe

Harriet Beecher Stowe moved from Connecticut to Ohio when her father, Reverend Lyman Beecher, accepted a job in Cincinnati. She met many escaping slaves when she visited her father's friend, Reverend Rankin. He told her stories about the slaves on the Underground Railroad. She aided runaways in Ohio and back in New England when she returned there. When the Fugitive Slave Act of 1850 was passed, an abolitionist newspaper published Stowe's articles about the awful ways slaves were treated. She also wrote an antislavery book, *Uncle Tom's Cabin*. More than 300,000 copies sold when it was published in 1852. It was translated into 37 languages. Everyone talked about her book. Legend says that when President Lincoln met Mrs. Stowe, he said, "So this is the little lady who made this [Civil War]."

This photo of the 127th Regiment, Ohio Volunteer Infantry (OVI), was taken in Delaware, Ohio, probably in 1863. The 127th Regiment OVI was the first completely African-American regiment recruited in Ohio.

The Civil War, 1861–1865

In 1860 Ohio helped elect Abraham Lincoln as the 16th president of the United States. Soon after he was elected, seven Southern states left the **Union** because they feared Lincoln would try to end slavery in the United States. Ohio remained part of the Union with other Northern states. When Southern **rebels** attacked Fort Sumter, South Carolina, on April 12, 1861, the Civil War began.

Many Ohio residents, especially those living closest to the slave states, went to fight for the South. They had moved to Ohio from the South and had family ties there. Many more Ohioans remained loyal to the Union. President Lincoln asked Ohio to train 13,000 soldiers. More than 30,000 men volunteered. By the end of the war in 1865, Ohio had sent the third largest number of soldiers of all the states, at 346,326. They lost nearly 35,000 of those men. Women in Ohio organized hospitals for the wounded, collected blankets for troops, and worked to improve conditions for soldiers. Women and children also kept farms in Ohio going while men were away fighting. Union Generals Ulysses S. Grant, Philip Sheridan, and William "Tecumseh" Sherman were all from Ohio. These were the Union's most successful commanders during the Civil War.

Ohio also contributed millions of dollars toward the war, much of it in the form of federal taxes, which went toward supplying Union troops. Factories in Ohio produced muskets, cannons, uniforms, shoes, tents, and other supplies for the Union army. Ohio packing plants sent meat to the troops.

Only two Civil War battles took place in Ohio. The Battle of Buffington Island took place in 1863. On July 13 of that year, **Confederate** Brigadier General John Hunt Morgan and his men, known as Morgan's Raiders, crossed the Ohio River into Ohio near Cincinnati, heading east in southern Ohio. Their goal was to disrupt Union war efforts by fighting and capturing soldiers, destroying bridges, and disrupting railroads. They were pursued by Union Brigadier General Edward H. Hobson and his cavalry. On July 19th, Union soldiers attacked Morgan near Buffington Island. It was a Union victory, but Morgan and 400 of his men managed to escape through the woods during the night.

Before John Hunt Morgan was captured in Ohio, he and his raiders destroyed 34 bridges and caused problems for railroads in 60 places on this raid.

Morgan continued east and north in Ohio, trying to find a safe crossing back over the Ohio River. Union cavalry chased Morgan and finally managed to cut him off near Salineville, Ohio. Morgan surrendered and was sent to prison in Columbus, Ohio, but he escaped in November of 1863.

Mother Bickerdyke

Mary Ann Bickerdyke, a nurse from Knox County, stands out for her actions during the Civil War. She became famous for the care she gave the wounded soldiers. They nicknamed her "Mother Bickerdyke" because of the comfort she brought to thousands of soldiers.

The Civil War ended on April 9, 1865, when the Confederate General Robert E. Lee surrendered to Union General Grant. In 1863 President Lincoln's Emancipation Proclamation had gone into effect, which freed the slaves in the states that had left the Union. Slavery was finally outlawed throughout the United States by the 13th **Amendment** to the U.S. Constitution, which was passed in December of 1865.

Growth of Industry, 1850–1900

During and after the Civil War, Ohio's industries continued to grow. Some cities, such as Akron and Canton, had factories that specialized in making farm equipment such as steel plows. This equipment helped women and children maintain farms while men were fighting in the Civil War. It also helped increase farm production after the war. By the mid-1800s, Ohio was producing more cereal grains, like corn and wheat, than any other state.

Mining also experienced a boom in Ohio in the 1800s. By the mid-1800s, many of Ohio's natural resources were needed to operate growing industries throughout the United States. Mining coal, **petroleum**, salt, sand, clay, and gravel became industries in themselves. Minerals, such as coal, heated factories and homes, and fueled steam engines. Thirty counties in southeastern Ohio became centers for coal mining.

Southeastern Ohio was especially rich in coal, and mines like this one near Pomroy, Ohio, helped fuel the state's industrial growth.

Iron ore mined from eastern Ohio helped make the steel industry important for the state. Iron furnaces were built, and towns grew as people came for work in the steel factories. Some cities, such as Youngstown, became very important producers of steel for the nation.

Having struck oil in nearby Pennsylvania and realizing the benefits of Cleveland's location on Lake Erie, John D. Rockefeller started the Excelsior Works refinery in Cleveland in 1863. He had his own pipelines and railroad tank cars bring oil to the Cleveland refinery. From there, oil-related products were shipped to ports in the eastern United States and on to Europe. Rockefeller founded the Standard Oil Company in Cleveland in 1870.

This is Standard Oil's first refinery in Cleveland in 1870. It is one of the most historic sites in the oil industry. The present Cleveland refinery is operating at the same location.

This man is taking samples from a railroad car full of sand, which is used in glass making, to check its quality. The sand is arriving at the Owens-Illinois Glass Company factory in Toledo, Ohio.

A large supply of natural gas was accidentally discovered around Findlay, Ohio, in 1884. This new, cheap fuel, which could be used to power many factories, further ensured that Ohio's industries in the region would thrive. Plentiful natural gas and deposits of sand, which are used in glassmaking, helped make Ohio a center for that industry. Edward Libbey, a glassmaker in Massachusetts, learned about the resources in Ohio from businesspeople in Toledo. He moved his factory and 100 employees to Toledo, where there was access to transportation and the natural gas and sandstone he needed to produce glass. He helped turn Toledo into the "Glass Capital of the World."

These men and women are decorating pieces at Weller Pottery in Zanesville, Ohio, one of the "pottery capitals" of the United States.

Ohio's supply of natural gas, together with large natural deposits of clay, also helped make the state a leading producer of clay products as well. Roseville, Crooksville, and Zanesville became pottery capitals of the United States. They produced ceramic stoneware used for pots, containers, and clay bricks. In the late 1800s, there was a great need for clay bricks for use in buildings, roads, and sewer systems. In the 1870s, more clay bricks were baked in Ohio than any other place in the United States. Many immigrants from England, Ireland, Scotland, and Wales found work in this industry in the late 1800s.

Benjamin Franklin Goodrich started the Anchor Fire Hose Company in Akron, Ohio, in 1871. His company made rubber fire hoses. At the same time, others were thinking of new uses for rubber, which could be made from the petroleum found in and around Ohio. Charles Seiberling founded the Goodyear Tire and Rubber Company in Akron, Ohio, in 1898. It grew with the popularity of the automobile and helped make Akron the "Rubber Capital of the World."

Rubber was not the only thing produced in Akron. Ferdinand Schumacher's Cascade Mills was the start of the Quaker Oats Company in Akron.

Ohio Inventors

Ohio's businesspeople built major industries, but it was Ohio's creative inventors who advanced technology in Ohio and across the United States. Orville and Wilbur Wright (right), from Dayton, Ohio, were the first to successfully fly an airplane. Thomas Edison, who was born in Milan, Ohio, invented many new products, including the electric light bulb. On a smaller scale, James Ritty of Dayton, Ohio, invented a "mechanical money drawer," and his business became the National Cash Register Company.

In 1879 the invention of Ivory Soap helped Procter and Gamble in Cincinnati become successful. Henry Timken **patented** his invention, roller bearings, which became an important part for modern vehicles. He moved his Timken Roller Bearing Axle Company to Canton, Ohio, in 1901.

Throughout the late 1800s, Ohio's businesses were booming. These businesses needed workers, and thousands of immigrants came from Germany, Italy, and Central and Eastern Europe to fill jobs. Ohio's population continued to grow, especially in cities, where most factories and large businesses were located. However, businesses often made profits at the expense of the average farmer or worker. A small number of business owners became wealthy, while farmers and workers—most of the population—suffered through low pay and unsafe working conditions.

Ohio Workers Organize

In the 1800s, farmers usually had to rely on railroads to transport their crops to markets, and the fares charged were often high. Farmers had no choice but to pay what was asked if they wanted to use the railroads. In 1867 a Minnesota farmer named Oliver Kelley founded the National Grange. It was an organization that worked to help farmers around the country. Its first goal was to get fair prices from the railroads to ship goods. By 1876 Ohio had over 1,000 local Granges with many farmers working toward that common goal.

More and more Ohioans worked in factories and mines as industries in the state grew in size and wealth during the second half of the 1800s. These ordinary working men and women faced difficult and often dangerous work, made low wages, and had no job security or health care.

Miner Strike

In 1884 coal miners in southeast Ohio went on strike for better working conditions. Owners brought in outsiders to continue working, so the strikers dumped barrels of oil onto coal cars, set them on fire, and sent them into the tunnels. This underground fire still burns today and has destroyed millions of dollars worth of coal.

Workers had little power to improve their conditions, since there were always new immigrants who needed work and were willing to take their jobs. If workers wanted **reform**, their only hope was to organize as a group. In 1886 Samuel Gompers and other labor leaders founded the American Federation of Labor (AFL) in Cleveland, Ohio. It worked to improve the lives of workers in Ohio and throughout the United States. The AFL eventually became the nation's most important labor organization. In 1890 another major union called the United Mine Workers was formed in Columbus, Ohio. In order to push reforms, workers sometimes went on strike. This meant they refused to work until their demands were met.

This photo of Samuel Gompers was probably taken in the 1880s, which is when he helped found the AFL.

The new labor organizations had some success in Ohio. For instance, Ohio was one of the first states to pass a law limiting the workday to ten hours. It was also one of the first states to recognize Labor Day as a national holiday. The new labor organizations also brought national attention to the business practices of the industrial leaders of the United States. Ohio Senator John T. Sherman sponsored a bill meant to reform big business in the United States. The Sherman Anti-Trust Act was made law in 1890. In 1892 Congress found Rockefeller's Standard Oil Company guilty of being a **monopoly**. The U.S. government broke Standard Oil into smaller companies so that there would be more **competition**. The federal government would now play a role in regulating American businesses.

Ohio Senator John Sherman was the younger brother of General William "Tecumseh" Sherman.

A Century of Growth for Ohio

In less than 100 years, Ohio had grown from a frontier state with 70,000 people in 1803, to an **industrial** powerhouse with a population of more than 4 million in 1900. Ohio's status in national politics increased at the same time as its economic status. Five Ohioans were elected president of the United States in the second half of the 1800s. One of them, William McKinley, was elected in 1896, and would take Ohio and the country into a new century.

President William McKinley helped guide the nation out of a depression. He was also president during the Spanish-American War of 1898, in which the U.S. was victorious.

Ohio Presidents of the 1800s

A total of five men born in Ohio served as president of the United States in the 1800s:

18th president	Ulysses S. Grant	1869–1877
19th president	Rutherford B. Hayes	1877–1881
20th president	James A. Garfield	1881
23rd president	Benjamin Harrison	1889–1893
25th president	William McKinley	1897–1901

Early 20th Century, 1901–1945

Efforts for **reform** in Ohio did not stop with businesses. Ohio's government suffered from corruption in the late 1800s, but a new reform movement began at the turn of the century. **Muckrakers**, such as Lincoln Steffens and Ida Tarbell, exposed the corruption of city bosses, such as George Cox of Cincinnati and Marcus Hanna of Cleveland. These men were millionaires who worked to protect their wealth. They bought the loyalty of politicians to do so, usually at the expense of the other citizens. Once the corruption was exposed, Ohio voters finally elected new mayors who brought respect to their city governments. Ohio voters also helped elect another Ohioan president. William Howard Taft of Cincinnati became the 27th president of the United States in 1909.

President William Howard Taft helped enforce antitrust legislation during his time in office (1909–1913). Taft went on to become the chief justice of the U.S. Supreme Court in 1921.

Floods of 1913

The worst floods in Ohio's history occurred during the spring of 1913. Unusually heavy rainfall in March of that year caused rivers to overflow. Most of the destruction happened around the Miami River, especially in Dayton. Over 400 people lost their lives, and the cost of damages was more than 100 million dollars. In 1914 the state **legislature** of Ohio passed the Conservancy Act. This act allowed flood-control dams and reservoirs to be built so that such severe flooding would not happen again.

World War I, 1914–1918

World War I broke out in Europe in 1914, and the United States entered the war in 1917. Over 200,000 Ohioans fought in the war. Soldiers trained at Camp Sherman in Chillicothe, Ohio, and pilots trained at Fairfield Air Depot in Dayton. A famous flyer from World War I, Captain Edward "Eddie" Rickenbacker, was from Columbus, Ohio. He shot down 22 enemy planes and 4 observation balloons to become the leading **ace** of the United States. Rickenbacker was awarded the Medal of Honor for attacking seven planes in one day on September 25, 1918. President Woodrow Wilson's secretary of war during World War I was Newton D. Baker, who was also from Ohio.

Ohio's factories also played an important role in the war. Factories in Dayton produced airplanes, Cleveland and Youngstown produced steel, and the factories in Akron produced rubber tires. Many factories were converted to produce trucks and tanks for the war, and many people came to Ohio for jobs in the factories. Ohio played its part in the U.S. victory, and World War I ended in 1918. The wartime production benefitted Ohio's economy, which continued to thrive until the Great Depression.

This is a 1918 photo of Edward "Eddie" Vernon Rickenbacker taken near Toul, France.

The 19th Amendment

Women had been working for equal rights and the right to vote since the 1800s. Finally, in 1919, the 19th **Amendment** to the U.S. **Constitution** granted women in every state the right to vote.

Great Depression, 1929–1939

The economic success of Ohio, and the rest of the nation, ended when the **stock market** crashed in 1929. This event signaled the beginning of the Great Depression. In Ohio 125 banks closed, and people's savings were lost throughout the nation. About 37 percent of the people of Ohio lost their jobs and could not afford food or house payments. President Franklin Roosevelt developed a plan called the New Deal. It set up agencies to help U.S. citizens work and make money. For example, workers in the Civilian Conservation Corps (CCC) earned money building Ohio's state and local parks, fixing roads and bridges, and improving the **environment** by planting forests. Another agency, the Works Progress Administration (WPA) created thousands of jobs for Ohioans and others around the U.S., including artists, who improved public buildings by painting **murals**. One of the biggest projects, started in 1934 and finished in 1938, was the Muskingum River Valley flood control project. In 1937 most of the dams constructed in this project held up to the heavy floodwaters of the Ohio River.

Life During the Great Depression

One Ohio great-grandfather was nine years old when the Great Depression began: "My father was an artist. He had a business decorating beautiful churches in Canton. He employed other workers. When the stock market crashed, he lost his savings and couldn't pay his employees. The bank closed. I remember my mother and father were afraid we would lose our house.

When President Roosevelt was elected, [his New Deal] helped my father. I remember my dad took his equipment and went to New York City. He painted the Radio City Music Hall as part of the WPA. CCC workers built a park across the street from my house. It's still there today."

These CCC workers are lining up fence posts in a soil conservation program in Butler County, Ohio. All materials were provided by the farmer.

Prohibition

Citizens who thought there was too much alcohol and too many saloons in the United States were called prohibitionists, because they wanted to prohibit, or ban, the production and drinking of alcohol. The Anti-Saloon League was founded in Oberlin, Ohio, and the National Women's Christian Temperance Union was founded in Cleveland. These groups worked for the passage of the 18th Amendment to the Constitution, which made it illegal to make or drink alcohol in the United States. In 1933 the 21st Amendment **repealed** prohibition, and alcohol could again be made and sold in the U.S.

World War II, 1939–1945

World War II began in 1939, but the United States did not enter the war until December 8, 1941. On December 7, Japanese bombers had attacked the U.S. naval base at Pearl Harbor in Hawaii. With a new demand for supplies, the war gave new life to Ohio's economy and brought the state and nation out of the Great Depression. Ohio farmers grew as much food as they could to feed U.S. soldiers. Ohio's factories once again produced tires, steel, airplanes, vehicles, ships, and ammunition. By the time the war ended in 1945, Ohio was once again an **industrial** leader in the nation.

Ohio factories required workers to help meet the demands of wartime production. African Americans came north to Ohio's cities for work. By the end of the war, African Americans made up more than six percent of Ohio's population. With so many men off fighting the war, many women had to fill the jobs the men left behind. By 1945 one of every three workers in Ohio's wartime industries was a woman. This experience paved the way for more and more women working outside the home in the second half of the 1900s. Ohio's contribution to the war effort was not only through its industries. About 840,000 men and women from Ohio served in the armed forces during World War II. When the war ended in 1945, Ohio's economy was **restored**, and its population was once again growing.

These four young women are putting together the dashboard of a Willys-Overland Jeep in a plant in Toledo, Ohio, on December 26, 1942.

Paul Tibbets

Paul Tibbets of Columbus, Ohio, was the pilot of the *Enola Gay*, the aircraft that dropped the atomic bomb on Hiroshima, Japan, ending the U.S. war with Japan.

Contemporary Ohio, 1946–Present

With the war over, returning soldiers were eager to settle down and build families. Many bought new homes in the **suburbs**. After the war, people had more money to buy cars and to travel. The increase in the number of people living in the suburbs led to more traffic and the need for wider highways. The Ohio Turnpike was completed in 1955, and other interstate highways began operating in the 1960s. Ohio's high birth rate and the continued **migration** of whites and African Americans from the South made Ohio the fifth most populous state by 1960, with almost 10 million people.

The growth of suburbs like this one outside Columbus (left, ca. 1950s) made the Ohio Turnpike (below) necessary for people to be able to travel more easily around the state.

Besides having the new interstate highways and the Ohio Turnpike, Ohio businesses also benefitted from the St. Lawrence Seaway, which opened in 1959. Oceangoing cargo ships could travel on the St. Lawrence Seaway. This meant that large ships could take cargo from Sandusky or Cleveland, travel directly from Lake Erie into the St. Lawrence River, which is connected to the Atlantic Ocean, and then to any port in the world.

Civil Rights

Almost 100 years after the Civil War and the end of slavery, African Americans in Ohio and around the country still suffered from **discrimination**. In 1959 the Ohio Civil Rights Commission was organized to protect Ohioans' **civil rights** and guard against discrimination. The Fair Employment Practices Law, passed in 1959, said that a person could not be discriminated against because of his or her "race, color, religion, national origin, or ancestry." Although there were laws in the state against racial **segregation**, towns throughout Ohio still practiced forms of segregation, especially in schools and housing. The Civil Rights Commission suggested making the schools racially **integrated**. Students were bused to schools outside their neighborhoods to create a better mixture of African-American and white students.

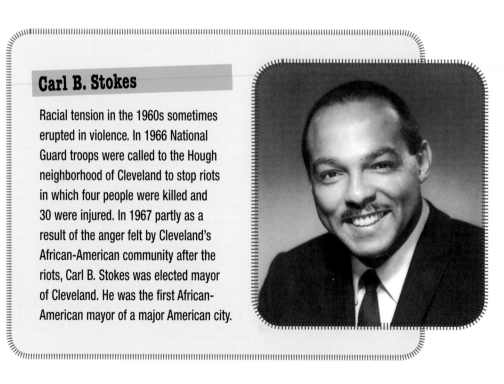

Carl B. Stokes

Racial tension in the 1960s sometimes erupted in violence. In 1966 National Guard troops were called to the Hough neighborhood of Cleveland to stop riots in which four people were killed and 30 were injured. In 1967 partly as a result of the anger felt by Cleveland's African-American community after the riots, Carl B. Stokes was elected mayor of Cleveland. He was the first African-American mayor of a major American city.

Space Race

When the U.S. entered the space race with the Soviet Union, Ohio made headlines. In 1962 Lieutenant Colonel John Glenn from New Concord, Ohio, was the first astronaut to circle the earth. Neil Armstrong, from Wapakoneta, Ohio, was the first person to walk on the moon on July 20, 1969. Space research was and is still conducted at NASA's (National Aeronautics and Space Administration) John Glenn Research Center at Lewis Field in Cleveland.

John Glenn poses here for a photograph in his pressure suit after being named as the pilot for the Mercury Atlas 6 mission of 1961, which made him the first American to orbit the earth.

Antiwar Protests

United States involvement in the **Vietnam War** (1957–1975) caused concern in Ohio and around the country. College students in Ohio and elsewhere protested against the war by holding marches and **demonstrations** at colleges and universities. In 1970 Ohio Governor James A. Rhodes sent National Guard troops to Kent State University in Kent, Ohio, to keep order. The demonstration ended tragically when the troops killed four college students and injured eight. The Kent State tragedy sparked further antiwar protests across the country and became a symbol of the divisions the Vietnam War was causing among American people.

Tough Times, 1970s

Heavy **industry** is what made Ohio great, but Ohio's industries, such as coal and steel, were less important to the national economy toward the end of the 1900s. Some companies, especially in the steel industry, closed because of lack of profits and tough foreign **competition**. The look of empty, rusted-out factories gave Ohio, the Midwest, and northeast regions the nickname "rust belt." Decades of heavy industry had also taken their toll on Ohio's **environment**. When a section of the Cuyahoga River, in Cleveland, actually caught fire due to oil pollution, Ohioans took it as a wake up call and made it a priority to clean up the state's environment.

Modern Ohio

Ohio's citizens have worked hard to clean up their state's environment, and great improvements have been made. In 2007 Ohio ranked among the top five states in manufacturing. The 2000 U.S. **Census** showed that Ohio's population had grown by over 500,000 people in 10 years. As the state moves further into the 21st century, its future looks bright. Ohio cities are cleaner and growing, and its people have celebrated over 200 years of Ohio history.

Ohio's Bicentennial

March 1, 2003, marked Ohio's bicentennial, or 200 years since it became a state. The Ohio Bicentennial Commission organized statewide projects, such as the Bicentennial Barn Painting. Each of Ohio's 88 counties has a barn painted with a red, white, and blue logo (right) to remind everyone of this historic event and the importance of farming throughout the state's history.

The Bicentennial Bell project provided another special celebration in each county. Making an iron bell like those that were used in Ohio during the early days of statehood was the highlight of each countywide festival. When Ohio became a state 200 years ago, bells were important and were used in Ohio schools, courthouses, and churches. These special bells have the date they were cast, the name of the county, and the Ohio bicentennial logo. The bells also serve as a tribute to Ohio's industrial history. These were just two of the many celebrations held during Ohio's bicentennial year.

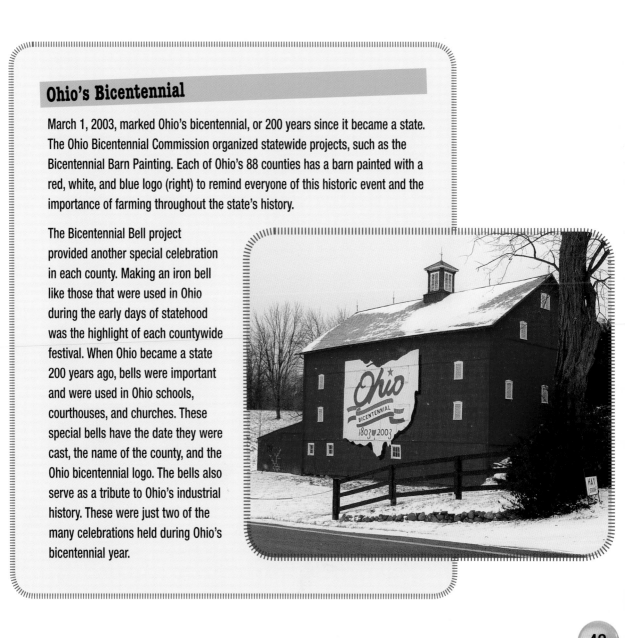

Map of Ohio

Ohio

Timeline

8000 BCE to 500 BCE	Ice Age ends; Ohio Archaic people arrive.
800 BCE	The early moundbuilders, the Adena and Hopewell, settle.
200 CE	Fort Ancient and Whittlesey people live in villages.
1756–1763	French and Indian War takes place.
1775–1783	The American Revolution takes place.
1787	Northwest **Ordinance** is written.
1788	Marietta is the first town in the Northwest Territory.
1794	Native Americans lose their battle against General Anthony Wayne at the Battle of Fallen Timbers.
1795	Treaty of Greenville moves Native Americans to northern Ohio.
1803	Ohio becomes the 17th state. The first library in Ohio is built.
1804	Ohio University opens.
1812–1815	War of 1812.
1825	National Road reaches Ohio; construction of Ohio **canals** begins.
1847	Railroads reach Ohio.
1861	Abraham Lincoln is elected 16th president; the Civil War begins at Fort Sumter.
1863	Lincoln's Emancipation Proclamation takes effect.

1865	Civil War ends; Thirteenth **Amendment** to the **Constitution** ends slavery.
1868	General Ulysses S. Grant becomes the 18th president.
1876	Rutherford B. Hayes becomes the 19th president.
1880	James A. Garfield becomes the 20th president.
1888	Benjamin Harrison becomes the 23rd president.
1908	William Howard Taft becomes the 27th president.
1917	The United States enters World War I.
1919	Nineteenth Amendment gives women the right to vote.
1920	Warren G. Harding becomes the 29th president.
1929	The **stock market** crashes and the Great Depression begins.
1932	Franklin D. Roosevelt becomes president; the New Deal helps Ohioans find work.
1941	On December 7, the United States enters World War II after Pearl Harbor is bombed by the Japanese.
1955	The Ohio Turnpike opens.
1962	John Glenn orbits the earth three times.
1969	Neil Armstrong walks on the moon.
2003	Ohio celebrates its Bicentennial.
2006	Ohio voters pass a statewide smoking ban in public places.

Glossary

abolitionist person against slavery

ace pilot who shoots down five enemy airplanes

allies people or nations united with one another in a common purpose

amendment change in wording or meaning in a law, bill, or motion

archaeologist person who studies the remains of past human life

arsenal place where military equipment is made and stored

artifact object remaining from a particular period

atlatl wooden tool with a hooked end used to throw spears

cavalry troops on horseback

canal narrow waterway made by humans and used for transportation

capital city where the government is located; a city known for a special trade or expertise

census count of the number of people in a country, city, or town

civil rights rights guaranteed in the U.S. Constitution

colonize settle in a new land

competition other side in a contest or match

Confederate soldier or person who sided with the South in the Civil War

constitution beliefs of a nation or state which establish the government and guarantee certain rights

culture ideas, skills, arts, and way of life of a certain people at a certain time

demonstration gathering to show public feeling

discrimination treating some people better than others without any fair or proper reason

environment surroundings that affect the way living things develop and grow

extinct no longer living

flint very hard stone that produces a spark when struck by steel

foundry factory where metals are cast

fugitive person who is running away or trying to escape

immigrant person who comes to a foreign country to make a new home

industry kind of business

integrate to make open to all races

legislature body of persons who make, change, or cancel laws

locks enclosure with gates at each end used in raising and lowering boats as they pass from level to level

mastodon large, extinct animal, similar to the elephant, with tusks and shaggy hair

migration moving from one place to another for food or to breed

monopoly complete control of the entire supply of goods or a service in a certain market

Muckrakers group of American writers, identified with pre-World War I reform and detailed written accounts of political and economic corruption

mural large picture that is painted or put on a wall

ordinance law or regulation specific to a city or town

patented protected by a document that gives an inventor the only right to make, use, and sell their invention for a certain number of years

pelt skin of a furry animal

petroleum similar to oil; oily liquid found in layers of rock in the earth

prehistoric from the time before history was written

prejudice negative opinion about a person or group of people based on incorrect information

rebel soldier who fought for the Confederacy in the Civil War

reform make better or improve

repealed do away with, especially by legislative action

reservation public land set aside for use by American Indians

resource something that is available to take care of a need

restore bring back to original state

segregation enforced separation of a group of people in society

stock market a place where parts of a company's worth, called stocks, are bought and sold

suburb settlement outside a city

surveyor people who measure the elevation and distance of land

territory area of land that is not organized as a state, but has its own local government

treason attempt to overthrow the government

Underground Railroad system in the U.S. by which people who were against slavery secretly helped slaves reach the North or Canada

Union Northern states during the Civil War

urban relating to the city

veteran person who has served in the military

Vietnam War (1957–1975) unsuccessful effort by South Vietnam and the U.S to prevent the communists of North Vietnam from uniting South Vietnam with North Vietnam under their leadership

woolly mammoth extinct animal, similar to an elephant, with shaggy hair and long tusks

Find Out More

Curry, Judson and Elizabeth Curry. *Regions of the USA: The Midwest*. Chicago: Raintree, 2007.

Edge, Laura B. *William McKinley*. Minneapolis, MN: Lerner, 2007.

Haugen, Brenda. *Harriet Beecher Stowe: Author and Advocate*. Mankato, MN: Compass Point Books, 2005.

Poulakidas, Georgene. *The Civil War*. New York: Rosen Publishing, 2006.

Roza, Greg. *The Adena, Hopewell, and Fort Ancient of Ohio*. New York: Rosen Publishing, 2005.

Santella, Andrew. *The French and Indian War*. Mankato, MN: Compass Point Books, 2004.

Index